Ann,

May these lead you closer
to God

Bro. Fred, S.J.

On the Road of Life
by Brother Fred O. Mercy, S.J.
Spokane, WA
© 2013

Illustrations by Fr. Andrew Wm. Vachon, S.J.
Front cover photo by Karl G. Corpron, used with permission.
Editing & Layout by Jere & Rick Gillespie, Columbiana,
2055 Chesaw Road, Oroville WA 98844.

All pen and ink drawings come from:
The Spiritual Exercises of St. Ignatius Loyola, S.J.
by Andrew Wm. Vachon, S.J. (Gonzaga University Press 1973)
Oregon Province Archives

Aspenels Printing has been an exceptional help in this endeavor.

Table of Contents

On the Road

O Lord, I know You are the Way, the Truth
and Life, but for now, I am lost.

I don't know where I am or where I'm going and
wouldn't know how to get there if I did.

Lord, rescue me from the blindness of my soul.
Bring me Lord into the Kingdom of Your love.
You know my desire and what keeps me from its realization
Act on my behalf with Your confident energy.

Guide me out of my jungle of false gods
Bring me from everything that binds me to nothing
Set me on that road that yields to me
Your healing ways, for my life
has been an undisciplined foray of one adventure
to another all ending in the valley of death.

So help me move to life as I can't accomplish this myself,
for I have continuously failed.

Oh, how great with me is Your patience;
How You wait, watching me stumble on
one bad road after another.
Where could I find such love?

Help me look toward you for that direction.
Help me, always, to be thankful as I begin
to experience the fruitfulness of Your road.

And let me always give You Lord
rather than myself the Glory and
Praise of following Your Road of Life.

Is There an Absence of Love

Where are You Lord?
Why have You abandoned me?
The atmosphere of my life
is loaded with despair.
Everyone wants a piece of me....
tugging at my property, tugging at my family.
My health is being drained before my eyes.
I am a forgotten carcass lying
helpless among the vultures.

And the medicine for my misery
swarms about me like flies around honey.
False mirages of hope and remedies
are constantly being held forth by my enemies.
The bars, the loan sharks offering easy money
and then, what seems the ultimate remedy;
that ideal man or woman who
just happens by at the height of my misery.

Oh, Momentary bliss!
How dear the price you extract for
that fleeting moment of ecstasy.

Is this how You treat someone You love?
Is this the inheritance promised to a faithful child?

What have I done to experience Your absence?
Why have You turned against me?

I would get mad except for precious reason.
Please prevail as my misery mounts.
I must, however, keep in mind
those past treasures, oh so numerous!

Help me Lord, to remember
in those seemingly centuries past,

How faithful You are to me.
I do remember You to be faithful,
never letting those vultures lick my bones.
I must remember that past, for it is the
only passage through this desert
of doom to that land of love.
I will remember Your wondrous
presence in my life, always supportive,
always the source of good.

Show Your face once again and
light the darkness that crushes my spirit.
Flush off the vultures.
Give life to my draining strength and renew
Your loving presence in my life.

I will remember the memories,
knowing their reality and live in their hope.

Why Embrace Oblivion

O Creator divine I am so lost.
It's not You who is absent from this relationship, but me.
Find me, O Lord, as I am lost in the forests of life
Seek me out O Triune God for I am buried
under the goals and ambitions of modern Humanity.

My thoughts and goals lie tied
to the desires of a lost people.
My work is building up
the passions of a wanderlust society.

O finder of souls, bring crisis to me,
which is the only experience I know that will draw
me away from the road I am following.
Awaken me, O Truth, from my ambivalent
acceptance of my walk towards death in a
culture enamored with its own creations.

You alone can make this happen.
Without this care for my good
I walk purposely towards oblivion.
I, like abandoned love, am walking in that obsession
that so distracts us from true love.

Only when I am sick enough,
will I cry out for help.
Only when Your creative crisis,
makes my commitment to Oblivion
make me begin to ask those questions
that will lead me to change;
leading me onto the right road.

Come, O Eternal Activist,
Guide me down Your path.
Lead me, such as I am,
to Your healing way,

To a love that is real,
To a love that grows
towards generative freedom.

Thank You, O Source of health,
For leading this wayward soul to Life

Why are There No Answers

Lord, Lord. Why haven't You heard my plea?
All day, all night I toil at this
Where are You, O Answer?

Impatiently I listen
And the air rings a melodious answer,
"nothing, nothing, nothing!"
My trial continues minute-to-minute, day-to-day.

O Font of Knowledge
Is my desire evil?
Is it too grandiose?
Is it something You're unable to give?

Change my deftness of Your answers to me.
Grant me the answer I know You want to bestow
Grace me to turn my anger and frustration
back to patience and love.
Strengthen my resolve to believe in Your Bounty;
Hear, Oh Lord, my plea.

Psalm of Creation

O Lord! Your presence surrounds me.
Every dawn the sun breaks thru the darkness
to illuminate Your handiwork.
You, Creator, can be found
everywhere on Mother Earth.

She shouts fourth in her joy of life from
the smallest to the greatest of creatures.
They shout out in their excitement of life.

Hosanna in the highest.... Blessed are You
who constantly gives breath to creation.

Continually keep the living in motion,
sending out Your existence that keeps us under
Your compassionate, life-giving watchfulness.

O Source of all energy!
Keep powering your corroded
and dying vehicles.
Oil us, wash us and protect us as a good
mechanic cares for his vehicle.

Let Your path to Paradise
seep into our blinded vision.
Break thru our feebleness to guide
our earthly cargo to the safety of Your Kingdom.

Destiny

O Lord, where are You when Destiny strikes?
You are surprisingly absent when tragedy overtakes me.
Life feels like it's abandoned me to the depths of hell.
Everything normal seems lost in the mirage of despair.

O Source of energy, why have You pulled Your plug in me,
Dissipating Your energy within?
Without You, my life teeters on the edge of the precipice of death.
Why have You abandoned me?
Where are You when I call?

Be patient, I hear a far-away voice from within.
"He will come; He will come"
And behold! He does! The Faithful One, the Source of Hope,
the Strength for the weak and forgotten.

You have broken through my prison of despair
You come in wisdom to comfort me in my dungeon of darkness
You are a light that pierces that darkest Destiny
Without You, O God, I would continue sinking in that
Mire of depression and death.

O Font of Health! Let me never forsake my Hope in Your Fidelity.
Let me always sing the praises of Your Love.
Let me trust in Your committed care for me.
Let my song of gratitude rise up to Your Holy Palace and
Reflect the joy of Your Presence.

Praise and Glory always to You, my God.
Amen, Alleluia.

Is Our Will Free?

O Creative Source, Sustainer
and Willer of everything.
To You I owe an unending thanks.
Everything that is good and
evil is allowed through Your Will alone.
How You respect my free will!
How You acquiesce to my decisions!

You love my free will so much
that You subject Yours to mine,
Making all things willed,
coming ultimately under Yours.
Who am I that I command this reverence?
What am I to deserve this respect?
Why then, oh why, do I so often
fling this gift back to You with such ease?

Why do I choose evil and then
seemingly stand around so unmoved?
One might think you would come,
with all Your power, and force me to good.
But No! That's not who You are.
You love Your gift to me so much
even to allow me to freely exercise it,
through the gates and into hell.

Where can I find this
same respect amongst us?
Create in me, O Lord, this same
respect for others and their will.

Lord, as You yielded to the will of others
and its consequences to Yourself,
Help me to imitate this, that
Your life might live in me as to
Make this part of You to be
Experienced again here on earth.

So, I will bless you all the days of my life.
With all my being I will always endeavor to allow
Each one's freely chosen acts that,
Eventually all of us, living in the light of Your Way,
will find ourselves operating in good
life-giving decisions.

18

Our Market-Place of Death

Everywhere I go Consumerism eats away at my flesh,
The enticement of a new car, a new radio or TV
Begs me to engulf myself in its poison
They beckon me by discounts,
No-interest paying loans and lottery tickets.
It's so hard to keep Your presence in mind amongst all this wealth
I look for You in all this accumulation of junk.
Your absence is as remarkable as Your presence in all this refuse.

Show Yourself, O Creator of good,
You are a way out through this jungle of materialistic pleasures.

I believe I can hear Your words amidst this cacophony of debris.
"Hang on, son! To My gentle, warming grasp of Freedom,
You can leave this desert of creative nonentity.
I will bring you to My Oasis of Simplicity.
There you will enjoy the Freedom of Plenty.
Taste and see how people and
relationships become more satisfying.
They cost nothing, but yourself and your beauty
For you are worth more than
The summation of all man's created things.

You are each other's salvation from this world of gadgets.
My hand must now be substituted for that of another
And together you find a way through;
A way out and into My Land of Simplicity and Freedom."

A River of Life

Lord! Your life flows on
like a river towards the sun.
Everywhere one looks,
one sees this flowing process.
So many of Your children never
see this same wonderful process,
But only opportunities for one's earthly gain.
Our lives then flow not gently and
reverently towards that sea of You,
But more like a gushing flood into a sewer.

See, how we, the children of the world,
work against Your natural process.
We pour the garbage of our
lives into the streams of life
We rape our forests for goods we call
precious but use once, then thrown away.
We steal minerals from mother
earth to create inventions of death

O Creator! Bring us back to where we
imitate Your Creating and flowing Love.
Draw us back to your flow of that
life-giving journey rather than that destructive
surge toward that eternal sewer of hell.

We swim in the world of things
and rather than gently flowing,
We sink abruptly into
the muck of death.

Help us to see the gifts of Your river.
Help us to see You in everything.
Help us gravitate towards The River of Life.

Where can I find God

O Lord! Let all creation
applaud Your masterful works.
Mountain so beautiful. Each time you
flex your muscle by a movement of your
glacier, you sing out, "Thank you God for my beauty.
I am dependent only upon You. All my strength
and beauty comes from You. I am much like that
great painting where thousands view my beauty,
then remember with great tenderness its master.
All I am then praises You, O master."

All of creation is music from You.
O Lord, I am in awe of Your greatness
and it's so evident in nature's total dependence
upon Your hand and Your life breathing
energy into it in Your ever-present concern.

Everything in nature is but one great
orchestration of Your composing genius.
It blends together all of nature's family.
It remains one great body of musicians
playing under Your direction.

How easy it is, Lord, to be touched
by Your composition in nature.
But Your greatest creative genius exists is myself,
but here it's so difficult to see myself as such.

I am diminished in my greatness,
because I lose that which nature
shows me so clearly. I refuse to be part
of Your orchestrating composition.
I want to compose my own music
and lead my own band.

My composition's become not of you, but of myself.
They become great Inter-continental Missiles,
Nuclear Powered submarines and all that creative
death that's born out of them.

My melody's become the cries of death
From the millions of the recipients of my creation's.
And the unrelentless battles of one
musician upon another.

My music is this refusal to allow Your
reflective image to make myself beautiful.

How hard I make it for anyone to see
in me a reflection of Yourself when I
constantly reflect my own desires, my own
compositions and my own music.

Can the mountain say to the sun,
"I'll not accept your warming rays or
I don't feel like moving my limbs this day?
So I'll leave my glaciers still today
and move them tomorrow."

"Oh rebellious Humanity! How I yearn to
have My instruments played in such a way that say",
'Thank You God for our talents. Praise You Lord
of Life, for all that I have comes from You
and my beauty is now more glorious and
resplendent than all of creation, for of all creation,
I am most like Yourself.'

For You are a God whose greatest
orchestration reaches its perfection in
Humanity, yet so seldom recognized as such by us.

Help me Lord to reflect Yourself in me.
Help me Lord, for I can not get there on my own.

Home

O loving God, always present,
Always yearning for my recognition,
You are the kernel of my being.
Yet I see myself as You....a god onto myself
It's me who sees the totality of myself outside of You.
I ignore the true essence or being of myself

Oh! How blind I am!
How set upon myself I've become,
that takes me out of reality and
Into that land of make-believe,
that swamp of selfishness and
quick-sand of self-destruction.

Rescue me, O Life Yourself
Bring me home to reality,
That place out of our selfish self,
Into that interdependent relationship of love.
Bring me home
To those pastures that give life
in a home of love.
Give way oh selfishness,
Give way to those fields of unreality.
Give way to that world of me.
Let Love be my home.
And let me rest in the warmth of yourself

I asked for strength that I might achieve;
I was made weak that I might learn humbly to obey.

I asked for health that I might do greater things;
I was given infirmity that I might do better things.

I asked for riches that I might be happy;
I was given poverty that I might be wise.

I asked for power that I might have the praise of men;
I was given weakness that I might feel the need of God.

I asked for all things that I might enjoy life;
I was given life that I might enjoy all things.

I got nothing that I asked for,
but everything that I had hoped for.

Almost despite myself my unspoken prayers were answered;
I am, among all men, most richly blessed.

Unknown Confederate Soldier

Choose

When I gaze at Your creation, I stand in awe
at its untiring and renewing beauty.
All around me are the constant
reminders of who You are.
And the greatest of these creative
geniuses is Humanity.
I am the ultimate in that
outpouring of grace and design.

But.....as I grow in wisdom and knowledge,
I begin to see debasement in Your creatures.
Violence has taken precedence over love
and self-indulgence over charity
I find myself searching in vain
for your Presence in a fallen culture.
Where are You O Life of Love?

I seem to be escaping into that vast world of things.
New cars, homes, mates and jobs that offer
a grand public image are the desire of my heart.
It's a world of glamour, money and power and
I don't need You Lord. I have more
than I need here and now.

Take pity on me Lord, for You can see
and recognize my catastrophe.
You know my weaknesses to
the things of this world.
Heed my call. Help me let you into my
life that I might truly see and let go of
this appealing world of nothing.

How foolish I am not able to see.
Can money, power and riches
give me what You can?
Can an incredible new and beautiful car
come anywhere near the effect of hearing

You say to me, "I love you and you give
me great joy when you hear and respond to me.

"Wake up, O Humanity! Where is your real
source of happiness? Open your eyes
to how the world of things is raping
you instead of loving you.

Which world do you want to follow?
One leads to death, destruction and slavery
and the other to life, love and freedom.

Choose!

Oh! Where have you gone, My Children?
I keep searching, begging and
longing for your return.
But, the time is nearing when
I will stop calling, stop searching,
stop yearning for your acceptance,
and simply allow your choice of slithering
into perdition, death and eternal darkness.

But know this! I will always hear
your call, even if it be but a whimper.
I will treat your plea as I would a
parched plant. I will give it the water of life.
I will tend to it, nourish it, sing to it and
gently bring it back to life, for I know
that behind that whimper is the yearning
for real life, for real love and for real freedom
from that world of things that will never,
never, never give the love that awaits you at the
beginning and end of your journey into love."

O Lord Answer Me

O Lord! Hear my prayer!

I come to You day after day,
night after night pleading for Your ear.
Surely You know I'm here....
surely my request is not unreasonable....
surely I stand in righteousness.

Why? Then, O God....Loving and
gracious God that You are....
has my petition remained dead?
Am I asking too much? Am I unworthy;

ungrateful or a too great a sinner?
What is it in me O God that displeases You?
Why can You not hear my plea?

"My child… Am I to be fitted into
a personality foreign to myself?
Am I so little understood as to
be put into such an image?
If you really want the answer to
your question, go to My Word.
As you experience Me in scripture
listen intently, for the answer you long
for lies within. I will come alive deep
within yourself and as you experience
this notice all the different people approaching Me.
Which of all of them is most like you?

Are you the rich young man? Are you the lady
who wanted only to touch my garment; the Centurion,
the Samaritan woman at the well? Were you one of the five
thousand following Me or did you remain
at home praying in the Synagogue?

Perhaps you can find no one to identify
with and perhaps in this void there lies an answer."

Lord… O Lord…! I believe I come to you
as a good child, but You know me better than I do…
Teach me bountiful Lord, Your ways that
I might stand rooted in Your love knowing
that I am loved.

Help me, O gracious God, to approach
Your eternal love in trust, humility and
confidence, yearning in hope for
Your giving self. Help me cling to
Your faithfulness in hope.

Praise to Your patient charity Lord.
Glory to You in Hope O Divine Answerer.
Thanks to You, O Divine Gifter.

Will it be Life or Abortion

Blessed be Your presence within me.
How I cherish this life I carry.
Tis Your gift to me that I must carry,
guard and nurture or it will die.
How many ways can I thank You.
In everything I do I will constantly
praise Your name for this life.

Help me that this life may reflect
the true image of You. Help me to feed
and nurture it; that it may radiate with a
shinning brilliance to dazzle every eye.

Praise to You, Father, Lord of all creation.

My heart will be a motivating force
of gratitude for such a gift. Live,
O Love, within me. Live to show the
world that such life is worthy beyond
any of our creations.

Who would kill such a gift? Many will try,
but only one has that limited power.
Yes, Lord! It is true! It is only I,
the containing vessel of this groaning
life who must say yes or no
to this living presence within.

Where are You, O Gifter of this new life?
Where are You as my insides cry out in
hunger for Your nourishment, Your counsel,
Your support, all so necessary for this life?
Why have You forsaken me? Do not leave
me in my anger. Do not leave me in my grave of despair.

If Your life within is to exist; if I must continue
to say yes to it, and continue as its Source, I need You.

Hear my cry, then, O giver of life. Hear my plea.
Do not leave me to the emptiness of sterility.

Lord, could not this great gift of life be also
the life of the Christ embodied within me?
Are you not life to the sterile, fullness to
the empty, and the match to any fire of true love?

Praise be to You, then, Lord Jesus,
for the gift of Yourself, the only real life for
anyone living.

On Silence

Praise to You, O creator of Silence!
Into this emptiness, I experience Your presence in awe.
O void of nothing! How stark and threatening
You are to those who know not Your precious Name,
who cannot experience Your overwhelming
presence in it's absence.

Glory to You, O loving God!

How can I not sing of the
happiness of such an encounter!
I'll break that negation with my

songs of exaltations to the wonder
of Your presence in that sanctuary!

Oh! The joy of Your presence in such
a setting, so confounding to most of humanity.
Those who sing and dance to the
noise of the world, know You not.
Those with blinders of consciousness,
to the debaucheries of love and inhibitors
of growthful creativity are like ones lost
in a forest. They have no clue
of the beauty surrounding them.

Help me to continue to open my heart
O essence of silence.
Help me to live in such a way as to
bring my ears out of their prisons
of clamor, noise and the constant
blare of material come-ons.
Bring me Lord to sing in that world of
emptiness; that song that, in Your Kingdom,
is a veritable symphony; that song of silence
wherein the Master Musician sings the songs
for those who can hear; those songs that are
enough to make Your children love You so much more.

Praise You Lord, in Your
domain of silence!
I will sing to You in constant
thanks for this gift to me.
Glory to You in this state of
being that Kings and Queens of
the world yearn for but never achieve.

It's Your faithful ones;
those living in Your love;
those who know and follow You
who are recipients of this gift.

Will It be Depression or Grace

O Lord…. I am crying out to you for help.
My life is filled with despair.
Every day I awake only to be frozen in life.
I sit for time unending unable to engage the day.
I sit not wanting to face the next moment.
I sit unable to talk myself away from this dying atmosphere.
Why can't I just get up and go to work?

I cry out, "Lord help me," but hear nothing.
Instead…. impure pictures fly across my imaginative vision.
Evil thoughts weigh in on my lost mind.
Where are you O fleeting Peace?
Why have you fled our home leaving it
vacant for any wind to blow through?

How might I extract myself from this mire of stagnation?
Where will I find the Hope I can call upon
to bolster myself up and out of
this weight of death bringing me down?

Then, from a far, I hear my name being addressed,
"Stand firm in your pleading!
Continue in Faith your petitioning.
Know, in Hope; that this time will pass and that a new dawn of
answers will lift you from that weight of death.
Love will rekindle life in your wounded self."

Your anchored negative emotions will react to that loving power
That pulls you free from that quicksand of depression, but
behind this magical experience is the Spirit of God.
How unexpectedly does it appear and….
It's not in the mystery of miracles,
It's not in the grandeur of angels, and
It's not in the power of kings or bureaucrats or agencies.

It is in the form of "Grace" in so many forms that knocks on the doors of my heart. Grace is in any form You come in. You might come as a doctor, a bum off the streets or sometimes as angel, but it is You, the one who hears my call and answers it.

Thank You, Lord, for your life in that person who hears my call. Thank You, Lord, for Your Grace and its power to rescue the lost. Thank You, Lord, for that Grace that allows one to hear those pleas and answers them.

Where are You, O God

O Lord! We are crying out.
Where are You? You who say You love us
in so many ways they can't be counted.
Show me! I am blinded in Your absence.
Where are You when we have no jobs
or food for our children?
Where are You when we are evicted
from our homes stolen by the greedy banks?
And what can we say to those questioning
our fate to the reality of the absence of Your Love
when they ask, "Where is your God?"
"And if this is the way He treats you, why would
anyone even consider Him as a loving Deity
much less pledge their lives to Him?"

We, Lord, are being physically violated daily.
Our foundation in Your love
flows out of us like a dying gasp.
Help our weakened beliefs.
O Lord! In spite of all this,
we cling in Hope.
We still lift our own broken

abandonment to You. Hear our cry!
O Lord! Help us to see!

See, it's not You
who pays us starvation wages.
See, it's not You behind that gun that,
through unjust laws, appropriates our houses and land.
See that its not You behind the
universal greed of the international rich.

So! Teach us, Lord, to pray for those behind the guns,
those who create political laws enabling greed to flourish
and bloom, those running multinational corporations
that systematically create and sustain the poor.

Help us, Lord, not to blame You
for the misery of the world.
Teach us, Lord, that the answers to these problems
comes through us who are reflections of Yourself.
Teach us, Lord, that it is we who must
not violate another with a weapon of force.
Teach us, Lord, that it is we who
must never, never pay slave wages.
Teach us, Lord, that we must never
be greedy in Your name.

Then, You Lord, in us,
will hear the cry of the poor.
Then, Lord, will the people experience
Your presence in us.
For You will come to us in one another.
Then we will find the answers to our
pain through Christ in each other.

Praise You, Lord!
Thank You, Lord, for Your existence
in our brothers and sisters who see us
crying out to You in our need.

Fill all of us, Lord, with this Life that will
be for the poor and for the lost what You want for them.
Send us, Lord, that we might truly be You for the World.

Why Allow Evil

O Lord of Goodness and Gifter of Life!
My soul cries out in a world full of such misery! Why?
Everywhere I look I see sickness, disease, anguish and death.

Why? Being so great, do You allow all this?
What reasoning exists to put so many of
Your children in the midst of a living hell?

Can You not hear the cries and anguish of Your children?
Tell me! Show me! I need to know or my
very being will rot in the absence of reason.

"My child! Look not to Me for such answers.
They exist right in front of your very nose.
I am a loving God. It is My very love of you that
limits Me from doing what we both see needs to be done.
You, would be the first to praise Me for lightening
these burdens but also the first to criticize Me when I
begin to infringe upon that sacred territory of your will.

See how you react when anybody attacks
your right to live the way you choose or requires
you to some formality that you don't want to do.

It's My respect for your will that allows you to do as you please.
It's not I who steals from another;
It's not I who commits adultery or creates
an invention that could erase humankind.
It's you. But it is also you who possess
the ability to use your will for good.
You can choose to lift the burden of the poor.
You can choose to rebel against war, greed and deception.
It is only your will that can alleviate the burdens of
the world and when you direct it that way, you will find
Me there beside you with all the help you need.

No...! My loving will, will only come alive in the world
when you bring your own acts of love into being.

I will never prevent you from making bad
decisions, that leads to someone else's suffering.

Help me to see this answer Lord, for it's so
hard to accept, much less see.

Praise you Lord for this light.
Glory to You Lord when I let Your will
become embedded into mine that I might
become Your answer to the world's misery.

Aloneness

Thank You Lord for your
presence in my life.
When I venture into life
and all its complexities,
You are there.

Sometimes I see You in the sunsets,
Sometimes I experience
You in the person next door;
Almost always in the stranger,
Everywhere I look I find You

I need not to feel lonely.
I don't need mass media and its
constant verbiage about nothing.
Nor do I need the warmth of a body
to make me feel secure from aloneness

You Oh Lord are a constant
presence, recognized or not.
Your presence is a constant
companion filling that gap of aloneness.

Is There Life in Death

O Lord! I seem to be frozen in time.
Time seems to fly past me as I seem
glued to this fading earth.
I cry out in my frozen body, "save me O Lord!"
Breathe your life into this body of ice.

Why, O Lord, have I lost my way?
What power has pushed me into this place
where the living seem to be harnessed to the dead?
Why do I feel like everything within
is set in perpetual un-motion?
I sit in the atmosphere of un-doing.
My soul lives in a grave-yard of the living.

This dream-like reality is so constant that it eliminates
even the thought of escaping into You.

"Get up! Awake! Get into Life" say those around me!
Finally…. In a last desperate cry
I whimper… "Rescue me, O Source of Life!
Come to me, Sustainer of the Living!
Save me, O Creator of every living atom
that is hidden within me."

For you are Love that motivates all life.
You are the Openness to the growth in all creation.
You are the spark behind every bonding
relationship into goodness.

Hear my cry for life. Let Your warming
hand warm this frozen body.
Thank you, Living Energizer for that electric charge
that moves me from death to life.
Help me, O Lord, to never forget
Who brought me back to the living.
Praise to you, O Eternal Life.

False gods

"Oh sinful Humanity!
How I long to draw you from the ghettos of your own despair!
How I wait for that fleeting moment of questioning
that so often slips past your garbaged life
leaving you forever in that oblivion of materialism.

It's into that world of cars....TV and sports
spectaculars....that life of soap episodes and that
idolatrous world of things that I yearn to pry.

Oh world of Humanity! Those treasures of aluminum and
plastic enslave you and become as gods onto themselves.

They draw you away from Me where as soon as they are
possessed they die only to give birth to next years models.
O Sweetest of Possessions! You are worshipped with such
passion only to become idols of which you can't be without;
idols that are a substitute for eternal joy.

Your world, oh Humanity, has been My gift,
but you've appropriated it onto yourself.
I am no longer the Appreciated Gifter,
rather some distant deity you refer to occasionally.

Oh that you might turn for but one
moment to see and experience life itself.
I am That whom your heart yearns for
yet I live among the vipers of commercialism."

Save me Oh God as I've been bitten
so much by the vipers of commercialism that my
system is adapting to its venom. Draw me Oh Lord out of the
whirl-pool of materialism that sucks me into that living hell.
If I don't have a new
car, a new house or get promoted, I am nothing.

Help me, O Lord, from this quicksand of mortgaged souls.
Lead me to Your people. Shepherd me into Your flock
which now lays scattered and vulnerable
to these modern-day wolves that devour all creation.
Sales-people, commercials, layaway and chance are their
names and they roam in packs preying upon Your flock.

Instill in me the courage to follow
Your ways into that pasture of free ground.
You know my weaknesses.
Send me Your strength that I might overcome
these modern idols for Your ways are not these false gods.

Your ways lead to freedom, truth and joy, and finally into
love where your loving, accepting presence
permeates every living tissue of myself.

A Touch of Love

O Lord! Your touch of
love is so constant!
It's always so near,
especially in Mother Earth.
In her trees continually
blooming forth every spring
as Brother Sun comes out
of his winter quarters.

O loving Energizer!
How much we must
remain in Your generosity.
How constant should be
our songs of joy for

Your breath of life!
More subtly than Your
generative power in Mother
Nature is Your gentle and
consuming touch upon us.
How much more personal
is this prevailing caress that
remains always an on-going reality
to those who know and
accept such affections.

How many ways are there to
thank You Lord for such devotion?
Are there enough songs of thanks
to give vent to such feelings of gratitude?
I can only beg of You, Abba.
Never let me slip into that swamp
of mediocrity where I accept Your
caresses as normal and mine by right.
Never permit me, Abba, to dissipate
into that state of lethargy where Your
touch becomes a right rather than gift.

Your touch is so continuous, Lord.
It portrays what no quantity of
words can ever express.
I love You Lord... and will live in
this continuing acceptance
of this caress for all time.

"You, in turn My child, can thank Me by
reflecting My happiness for all the World to see.
For just as two lovers are oblivious to their
surrounding world, that world is not to them.
That world can see the result of those signs and the
resulting happiness they bring to each other.
So must it be with you, my loves. The world must
see My loving touch and its effect upon you.
In this way, will your thanks be complete."

Praise You Father and thank You, O Loving Caresser!
You will remain forever that love consuming all Humankind.

The Battle Against Myself

Blessed be You God,
True protector of Peace.
For You, in the thickest of my
battles, never leave me,
never abandon me to myself.

Even in my darkest hour,
with adversity choking off
Your life-giving support systems,
I know You always to be near.
You are just waiting for those
sieging troops of despair
To weaken and let You break through with
Your replacements of replenishing hope.

Oh! What a mistake the enemy makes
retreating in despondence to that land of self.
This arid land is full of pitfalls
with a deadness and absence of light.
This eternal wandering in the emptiness
of the land of self is but one more step away
from that path to victorious peace.

With You, however, as light and general
I will forge out of that enemy territory
those areas of quicksand, darkness and
unto the high and lighted ground of Your Kingdom.

Here I see clearly the snares and
pitfalls of modern warfare,
for it's no longer my ground but Yours.
Your fortifications are solidly based in truth.
They are all easily defended,
with walls of fidelity, trust and hope.

They remain impregnable to the
forces of selfishness, deceit and despair.

What a blessing exists when I remain
committed to that correct path of battle,
for I know the victory-bound road I travel
and trust the general directing the campaign.

Oh! The love that such a faithfulness creates.
My being sings out chants to Your majesty.
Drums beat deeply within my heart
which is but one response to Your presence as Leader.

What forces can keep me from the victory of love?
There can be none that can separate me from Your Strength.

On Angels

Praise to You, O Masterful Creator!
From Your bountiless imagination
grew those endless choirs of angels.

Pure spirits they surround everything that
physically enshrines we humans.

Singing out that constant melody of harmonious praise
in thanks to Your creative genius, they are at Your
beckon and call, and without thought respond.

Thanks to You, O Eternal Ruler Divine!
For You have given my guardianship
to my protector, Your angel.

Let my song, then, be joined to theirs
that together we might chant our thanks
for Your sustaining, sanctifying and loving care.

A Plea of Need

Thank You Lord for who You are.
You always hear my pleas.
Your ears are as open to me as
any mother to her whimpering child.
Your answers are as a blanket on cold winter nights.
Your gifts are as welcome as the morning sun.
My entire being, if but more open to Your love,
would radiate myself as a continuous poem of gratitude.

But! Lo! I am such a self oriented being.
How easily I appropriate onto myself Your gifts.
Only to loose sight of You the Gifter.
Absorbed in self, I create my own
universe of graduated darkness till,
enmeshed in the muck of my own reality,
I come to that awakening that
I'm drowning in my own excrement.

"O Lord! Where are You", I whine
as if You had abandoned me.
"Come to my rescue", I demand even as
every babe cries for its milk.
As that mother yields her breast to that unthankful,
demanding and loud creation of Your love,
so You Lord yield Your presence to my need.

Again and again this cycle persists.
Help me Lord to stop this cycle.
Help me Lord to not let my eyes,
my ears and mind love You in times of need only.
Help me Lord for even though I inhabit this
adult body; think I possess a controlled and
disciplined mind and claim sanity, I am still but
an unthankful, loud and demanding child.

How many ways can I thank You for Your patience?

Teach my heart, O Lord, to explode with the power
of the atom and send out shock waves of gratitude
to You as Gifter in good and bad times ..

Bind me, O Lord, to that Hope that I will not abandon You.
Claim me, O Lord, for my faithfulness to that continuous thanks.
Proclaim me, Lord, to Your Way that forgoes my own.
Name me, Lord, as one obedient to Your love.
Praise to You, Gifter of Life!
Glory to You, Sustainer of Love.
All power to You, wondrous and mysterious sustainer of gift.

Rescue Me...

What is this dread that surfaces within me so often?
Is it not that space in me that still clings to the ways of Humanity?
That space that still remains all mine;
that territory still off limits to You, O Lord.
Leave me not to my own ends, O Lord,
for here is where all Humanity lives in failure.
Let me not be victim to my own strength.
Guide me despite myself to where all love is settled.
O Lord—How we cling to all that leads to death.
Help me, O Lord, to cast off these old ways that lead to nowhere,
for I am weak and need so to call upon Your strength.

You never fail to hear my plea, O Lord.
You are always there to lift me out of my own quicksand.
You are faithful in ways I can not even understand.
Let my thanks be raised through this despair
to lay in hope before Your goodness.